Babel's Daughter

◈

From the Bible Belt
to the Holy Land

Dear Miriam,
Shine On!
♡
Chaya ח

CHAYA LES

DEDICATION

To my beloved children - Yeshaya, Beriah & Maayan

Dear ones,

Here sits the story of how you came
to be born in the Land of Israel.

I may be Babel's daughter
but it is up to **me** to chose
whose sons & daughters you will be.

And so I chose for you to be
first-generation Israelis
Jerusalem-born and bred
and fed on the true wonder-bread
of finally coming home after an
epic wandering trek.

You, my children,
will bask in Mediterranean sunsets
You will be the masters of 2 languages
and poets of many inner-tongues.

You will radiate as only a child of Zion can
born back into the mountainous Judean

Reaping the legacy of the legions of priests
and priestesses who have walked before you.

You will weep over her wars.
You will mourn her losses

and celebrate her gains.

You will invest wisely
in the stock of humanity & humility,
in the stock of holiness and of family.

You, dear children, will always be
all that G!d can be
when put neatly
into the petite
container of a child
in the late 5700's
at the tingling feet
of Mount Zion.

The latest lions
in the Lester line
newly founded in
the land of Promise
to a mother and father
both children of Babel
who chose to make you
children of Israel.

◈

CONTENTS

Dedication

Acknowledgments

Orientation — Pg 8

Opening Prayer — Pg 15

Chpt 1: The Babble Belt — Pg 20

Chpt 2: The Mystic — Pg 33

Chpt 3: Jerusalem Fever — Pg 45

Chpt 4: Aliyah & Yerida — Pg 61

Chpt 5: Integration — Pg 76

Further Readings — Pg 92

About the Author — Pg 124

Praise for "Babel's Daughter" Show — Pg 128

ACKNOWLEDGMENTS

Even for a wordy person like myself, it is a challenge to adequately acknowledge my precious husband, Rav Hillel, for his many multiple thousands of moments of partnership, encouragement and steadfast support. How do I enumerate all the forms of assistance you have given – technical, philosophical, artistic, inspirational?
Hillel, you have been my mainstay and my rudder.
More than that, you have been the wind that moves
me forward and the very water in which I sail.
You are elemental to me. This one's for you my dear:

Hillel

A man committed to raisin' up children.
Raised up like a kiddush cup
not afraid of getting drunk.

Over-spillin', G-d-willin'
nachas-from-the-little-ones
A Rabbi, a therapist
a good guy, a real mentch.

And did I mention
full of vision
gentle sort of hierophant?

G-d-centered, meditative
California – elevated.
Torah-talkin', kosher-keepin'
Mystical, but with good reason.

A builder of Israel
inner and outer
attitude and latitude
because both matter.

*

And then there are my wonderful parents – Gary & Cheryl Kaplan. Another daunting task when it comes to expressing adequate appreciation for the innumerable forms of support you are to me. I will never forget that Friday night, sitting on the living room couch, when you simply insisted that I *must* keep on writing. I was ready to be done with it all. Until you and Hillel did a little intervention that set the course for this creation.

But there have been so many such nights, days, years, lifetimes of your caring, direction and love. I am so incredibly blessed to have you as my parents, my teachers, my good friends, my wise guides (Dad, that's your cue for comic relief).

I also want to acknowledge my fabulous parents-in-law – Eli & Shayna Lester – for your love, your song, your vision, your good works and good counsel. And to my mother-in-law Sue Parker – for your sweetness, humor & love – and for letting us use your RV for our first U.S. teaching & Babel's Daughter tour! And to Grandma Gloria for your wild spirit & sweet support.

My brother, Brad Kaplan, thank you for your wisdom, humor and creative perspective. Your powerful influence on me fills the pages of this book. Ellen Kaplan, your encouragement and enthusiasm for this show have been enormously meaningful for me. Thank you for your modeling of motherhood, your questioning, your contagious positivity.

And to the rest of my Memphis family and friends who were such big parts of this story of my growing up and beyond. The wonderful Grandpa Norman Kochman, Michael & Judy Edelson, Judy McCowan & Pete Lemon, Sandy Armus. Henry & Norris Marcus, Bob & Carol Pinstein, Kay & Shelley Sazlowski, Mimi Grossman, Mike & Michelle Less. Of course, my beautiful childhood friends Caroline Berz, Ashley Herrod, Clare Burson, Rosie Abell, Lindsey Chase & Brooke Mosely.

My mentors & teachers: Rabbi Wayne & Ellen Dosick. Rabbi Eli Spitz. Peter Pitzele. Jennifer Laszlo-Mizrahi. Dorit Bat-Shalom. Rabbi Daniel Kohn. Rabbi Zalman Shachter-Shalomi. Thank you all for your brilliance, trail-blazing & belief in me.

I am so blessed with a community of common souls in Jerusalem, where I am lucky to call my teachers my friends.
Rabbi Joe & Rolinda Schonwald, my mama and papa archetypes in Israel for so many years. I have loved every minute of it. Such a gift to have you as mentors. Rabbi Sholom & Judy Brodt, my neighborhood tzadikim, for modeling righteousness.

Rav Aaron and Miriam Leibowitz, for your unending depth, vision, sweetness and community building. Gary & Leah Levitt for your steady positivity, grace and belief in us. Jody Feld, for your modeling of what it is to be a holy Jewish woman. Sarah Yehudit Schneider, for your potent channel of teachings that are at the core of so much of my work.

To Jenna Alpern for your tireless & fabulous work creating and sustaining the Shalev Center. Ariella Amshalem for your sharp wit, sharp eye and soft neshama. Michael Kaye for your comic additions. R'Dave & Chana Mason, for your entrepreneurial genius & generosity. And to Andrew Tertes for the wonderful creative partnership of Sapphire Ink Press.

Also deep appreciation to R'Moshe & Leah Hesed. R'Raz & Leah Hartman. Nati & Michelle Cohen. R'Ami & Eliana Silver. Aliyah Fragen. Ilana Nelson, Maskit Ben Moshe & Sheva Chaya Serveter – for your sacred friendship. To my Berkeley sisters and all the ladies in my women's groups – present, past and future.

Finallly, to all of our friends and students who have come through the Shalev Center. It is a joy & honor to witness and work with each one of you.

BABEL'S DAUGHTER – THE SHOW

The book form of "Babel's Daughter" is taken off of Chaya's electric one-woman show by the same name. This book takes the script of that show and expands it into a more nuanced and robust poetic memoir of Chaya's journey.

Although Chaya's journey is a Jewish one, the themes and lessons woven together in this book are universal and reflect an archetypal spiritual quest.

Chaya performs the show regularly in Jerusalem at the Shalev Center. The show is a delight for audiences of all religious persuasions. Chaya also tours with the show.

For more information about coming to see Babel's Daughter live in Isreal or bringing it to your community please visit:

WWW.BABELSDAUGHTER.COM

ORIENTATION

As we begin, a little orientation is in order. First off, at the very root of the word orientation is the 'Orient'- the East - where the sun rises, the first rays of light, the locus of beginnings.

I did doctoral work in Jewish Studies at Oxford University in England for several years. Inevitably I'd get asked, "And what department aaawe you in lassie?"

I'd answer, "Oriental Studies."

"Whot!? Whot's a religious Jewess like you doing studying the Oooorient?"

"Well, old chap, Judaism *is* an Oriental religion," I'd respond.

It's true. Israel is in Asia, y'all! Now, I ask you, what images comes to mind when I say the 'Orient'?

The answers I usually get are things like bonsai trees, meditating Buddhas, steaming pots of green tea. Okay, so there's a little smog in Bangkok, but for the most part there's a lot of close-eyed serenity that comes to mind when people think of the Orient.

Now, what images emerge when I say "the Middle East"? Blown-up buses, skies full of smoke plumes, images of angry young men flinging rocks? The Middle East, in our imagination at least, is nearly synonymous with "conflict." Strangely, the imagery for the Orient and the Middle East are almost opposites.

Let's just for a moment let that "Middle East" baggage drop and insert some of the "Oriental" images into our vision of what the Holy Land is and could be. Let's orient ourselves to the Orient - to a more internally minded framework.

INNERTAINMENT

For that is what this story is about. It is about sharing a more oriental, a more inner-directed, vision of Israel as a land of the spirit rather than as a land of conflict.

This story is not just entertainment...it is what I like to call *inner*tainment. For your task here is to read with an eye to *your* insides. This piece of innertainment strives to illuminate *your* inner journey while reading about mine. Our orientation is an orientation to our inner selves.

I pray that you will hear your own story in the echo chamber of mine. And that the details of my spiritual quest, will merely serve as a spring-board & looking-glass for your own.

*

There is a story that Rabbi Lawrence Kushner tells of teaching a Sunday school class of children. They go on a field trip down the hall to the synagogue's sanctuary. When they arrive, Rabbi Kushner points to the lavishly curtained arc and asks them, "So, what do you think is behind that curtain?"

The children call out, "A palace." "A brand new car!" "Some sort of Jewish book." And one child, poignantly, gazes upon the curtains and answers, "A mirror."

For Rabbi Kushner, and I would agree, it was that last answer that best hit the mark. For the Torah, the Bible, at its highest, is a mirror. It is a method by which we see our own hitherto hidden faces.

At Revelation, the epic giving of the Torah upon Mount Sinai, the text tells us that all the people beheld God, face to face, *panim el panim*. The commentators say that this was "as if they were gazing into water". For what happens when we look into water? Wonderfully, we see ourselves!

The Torah is an archetypal reflecting glass - a watery substance whose very essence allows the text-beholder to behold themselves...and in the process, to behold the Divine.

So, too, this book, at its highest, aspires to hold up to you a mirror. The *point* of this story is to *point* to you.

Your Job: Read and REFLECT.

THE PASSPORT

Now you may be wondering, "Great theory Chaya, but how do I do that?"

Here's how. Whenever I perform Babel's Daughter, at the outset of the show, everyone in the audience receives a pen & a little blue passport. I call it "the passport to your Inner Israel". The audience uses this "passport" as a writing pad throughout the show. This book too can be like a passport for you, as you embark on your own inner journey.

There are going to be several stops along the way of our journey together. I call these *mirror moments*. At different intervals throughout the book we will have mirror moments. I will pose a question to you. This is your chance to stop and hold up a mirror to yourself. To be a tourist, touring the terrain of your *Inner Israel*.

Write out, in free association, whatever is coming up for you. This is not to be belabored. The best thoughts are the first thoughts.

Allow your hand to write out whatever is coming up – without judgment. As I like to say, "Non-Judgment Day is Near!"

This is for no one else to see but you. So be real. Israel is real!

INTERNAL COMPASS

So inquire and see,
where has the Holy land landed in thee?
Your internal compass
is the one text I compel you to read.

YOU yourself are the fibrous
flesh of God's tent.
Instructions for construction
are engraved on your skin.

YOU are the blueprint for building
- Unfurl!
For the study of yourself
is the map of the world!

MIRROR MOMENT:

Your first assignment: Every passport opens up to a photo. Below do a sketch of yourself. A one-minute sketch, with a word or phrase underneath it describing your inner state right now as you are beginning this book. (Examples: open, curious, riled-up, tired, etc. Or you could get more creative – The Visionary, The Skeptic, The Exhausted Mother)

PASSPORT

מרכז שליו
SHALEV CENTER
Pioneering Jewish Personal Growth

State of
Inner Israel

OPENING PRAYER

(BEFORE THE BEGINNING)

To start off this journey I begin with the common starting point of all of our journeys – Before our souls even set foot onto the terra firma of time and space, birthplace and name. It begins within…in the womb.

The Talmud teaches that each of us learns the entirety of Torah while in the womb. There is a candle lit above our invetro-souls and in the drench of that lamp-light an angel teaches us the entire Torah. At our destined hour of birth that self-same angel touches us above our lips, as if to say *shhhhh*, creating the gentle slope of indention known in anatomical parlance as the philtrum.

With that touch we forget all that we have learned in our 9-month tutorial. Life sprawls out before us as an on-going uncovering of all we have forgotten. Each piece of Torah learned is thus imbued with a striking sense of deja vu, of resonance with a truth we have seemingly always known.

Next time you look at your own face in the mirror, see that indentation…and be reminded of the Sinai of the womb, of the Torah that you have carefully tucked away.

And so I open this journey with a prayer from the womb. It's a prayer of all of our pre-born souls…on the cusp of life. It is a prayer that we can all recall the Sinai lamp-lit teachings of our own beginnings.

SINAI INSIDE

Touch me lightly 'neath the nose
That my lips may part in prose.

Let me not forget You
though I fall into the world.

Let luminescence last me still
and still my hearts with seraph quill
if I fall too far to hear
& memorize your notes.

Send a script- A scrap of timber
A stub of finger equipped with a pencil
May my new-born have utensils
to inherit as she grows.

And I will write
what I have learned here,
in this hollow, warm and light-filled.

So touch me slight
that I may recite
all that the angel quill
inscribed upon my soul.

And from this amniotic Sinai
I will find the voice to cry the truth
though all the world would call it lies.

And though I fall insane, forgetful
-- slap my lips and snuff my candle
yet I will remember well the angel
that taught me all I know.

And marked thus with indentation,

16

I will recall the revelation
of this loom where God wove
with love my soul.

For Sinai stands indelible
above our lips
to tell of all that we forget,
as sure as we are born.

So let us thus pursue Your truths in deja vu
wrap us well in what we knew
there in the womb.

And Israel will be as a mother
enfolding us to rediscover
the radiance lost in the rubble
of our own forgotten Truth.

MIRROR MOMENT:

Imagine yourself in the womb in that angelic lamp light. The angel is about to touch above your lips. She says she will allow you one thing to remember. What is that one thing?

_____

_____

_____

_____

_____

_____

_____

_____

_____

_____

_____

_____

_____

_____

_____

_____

_____

_____

_____

CHAPTER 1

THE BABBLE BELT

I was born into this latest migration of the Jewish nation, from European provinces to the promises of a new land of ultimate opportunity. I was born—1974, Cary Renee Kaplan. Memphis, Tennessee.

Memphis, the very buckle of the Bible Belt. But wait, we must pronounce it correctly, in proper Southern. Here's the trick to *speakin' propa Southern.* You put on a big saccharine smile and elooooongate all your vowels. Now say it with me, "Baaaable Belt."

That's right, in proper Southern, *Bible* comes out conveniently as *babble.* Babble, as in "speaking incoherently", a meaningless cocktail of words and sounds.

Babble, as in "the Tower of..." The Tower of Babel, is the biblical archetype of jumbled speech and mixed up identities. The word *babel* is culled from the Hebrew word *bilbul,* meaning confusion, being mixed up, stirred together, intermingled. America stands as the epitome of *bilbul,* the mixing bowl, the melting pot/tossed salad combo. This place where all are welcomed—stirred-up & stirred-in.

The Bible I learned in my buckle-belting youth was more babble than Bible, more Christmas than Hanukkah, more spin the bottle than spin the dreidel.

For instance, as 'Jewish' as I get, no matter how many scarves I wrap around my head, no matter how long my hem, no matter how many times in one conversation I close my eyes and say *Baruch Hashem*[1], still, when I stub my toe, I let out an irrepressible howl of "Jeeeeezus Christ!" Like a natural reflex! It's an all-too-telling Americano-evocation of the god of stubbed toes and other small inconveniences.

And perhaps that shouldn't be a problem; a little unconscious slip of the tongue never hurt anyone. But, I am a big believer in making the unconscious conscious. So a subtle under-the-breath call out to what is after all a foreign god is no small incident for me. It is a moment of ultimate *bilbul*, of confusion, an unconscious mixing and stirring, and foreign infusion. It is a twisting of tongue from mother tongue to other tongue...where identity is undone.

---

[1]Baruch Hashem is a Hebrew term meaning "Thank G!d" that gets used incessantly in religious circles. It is the perfunctory religious response to "How are you?"

EGYPTO-SOUTHERN WASTELAND

But let's get back to Memphis, the stage upon which this story is set.

Memphis Tennessee begot her name from no less than the first royal city of Egypt. The original Memphis stood majestic along the Nile River, just as my Memphis sort of slouches against the great American Nile—the Mississippi. Memphis even once had a football team called the Pharaohs.

If there was ever a team destined to be defeated this was it! A little hint to the wise, never name your sports team after THE biblical archetype of the bad guy defeated by a pack of slaves! Why tempt God?

And speaking of destined for failure, there's the famous Memphis Pyramid. Or not so famous. It's this massive glass pyramid, planted there along the river. A building which went from a failed concert/sports arena to a mega-church to now housing - a Bass Pro fishing shop.

"That's right y'all, servicing all your fish pole and handgun needs. Like the great pyramids of lore, made to represent the sublimest ideals of Egyptian culture, so too the Memphis pyramid now stands as an icon of the highest of Southern heritage – huntin' and fishin'!"

A pyramid with a sharp-point, but otherwise rather pointless. Although I suppose it does have one very poignant point for me, personally. It's my very own larger-than-life standing symbol of my 'leaving Egypt'. From the Mississippi Delta to Delta airlines –

Flight #322, Memphis to Atlanta to Tel Aviv. Where you age 40 years in the span of just 18 grueling hours of international travel!

The perfect stage from which to launch my own epic reliving of my ancestral freedom march, from slavery to the Promised Land!

And so it was with a strong hand, that I was plucked from my Egypto-Southern wasteland.

THE REBEL

But all that bad-mouthing of Memphis is really an exaggeration. It was - actually - quite a lovely childhood there in suburban South. Idyllic even. Held cozy in a quaint Jewish community of upper-middle class means. I remember petting ponies on my morning walks to Riverdale Elementary. Baskin Robbins every weekend, JCC camp every summer. I even went to the same high school as my mother.

Oh, and I played out the American high school dream to a T -- was a cheerleader, class officer. I even reached the apex of the social pyramid – being crowned White Station High School Homecoming Queen (I can die content!).

But as much as I excelled in blending-in, got all A's in my 'assimilate yourself' classes. I was still unavoidably a yid[2]...still got bat-mitzvahed and paid my dues at Hebrew School.

Though, I must admit, my favorite part about Hebrew school was break-time – which we might as well call 'break-the-law' time. Every Wednesday we were this herd of Jewish nerds migrating across the street to Kroger's grocery.

My highest Hebrew school aspiration - to see how many lipsticks I could slip into my backpack. Hebrew school for

---

[2]Affectionate term meaning "a Jew".

me was little more than the start of a successful career in shoplifting, or smoking clove-cigarettes, or any number of sundry acts of teenage rebellion.

Judaism was just another thing for me to gleefully rebel against, and I was a glutton for anything rebellious. By age 15, my one rule was to break the rules....in a middle-class sort of way. You know, shop-lifting, downing untold numbers of wine coolers in the Arby's parking lots, even once jumped a railroad train straight across the Mississippi River to Arkansas.

All I wanted was so to break, break out, break through...out of all the many claustrophobically comfortable encasings of my upbringing.

Comfortable is the operative word here. For my childhood was all about comfort. From the comforts of financial security to the comfort of cultural conformity. I saw my parents world as the kingdom of the comfortably numb...

COMFORTS ARK

If there ever was a Bible character who epitomized comfort it was Noah. For Noah's name in Hebrew literally means 'comfort.' "Noah's Ark" could better be read as "Comfort's Ark." An apt term for any type of structure that we build around ourselves to be like a shell of protection.

Look at Noah; the world was on the verge of ecological extinction (sound familiar?) and Noah's response—a well-insulated escape vessel. He didn't try to change the world around him but rather built a casing of comfort—comfort's arc—and for this he garners considerable criticism from the Bible commentators.

And I would have readily agreed—for in the wash of my teenage hormonal angst, I was set upon rejecting my parents carefully constructed arcs of comfort. What I wanted was to plunge into the waiting deluge of the world—no matter her pains. I wrote this poem about my the synagogue of my youth when I was eighteen.

ARK ANGEL

The synagogue of my youth
her sanctuary was my ark
it arched above my bowing head
its wood was rich and dark

My eyes would rise up ceiling's curve
which like a wave's soft back
bulged with the waters of our prayers
which crashed on heavens black

We sat in twos or family fours
like creatures far from home
while thirty feet into the air
ark's belly was our dome

Our needs were met as sure as breath
is given by G-d's wind
our prayers were by attentive ear
heard ere we need begin

Like flight of birds our voices rose
within this vessel cage
yet, just outside the sound was heard
of a world in stormy rage

And at the apex of the roof
of our inverted ship
a window round of painted glass
let fall a single drip

The dagger drip cut through the void
of our sustaining womb
sliced through the prayer that filled the air
anointing me with doom

For this small taste which wet my face
with water of the world outside
could penetrate and transform space
like the tear of an angel's cry

And all that was once safe and sure
transformed before my eyes
into an overbearing storm
of sharp and fiery lies

Beneath the bonds of beams of wood
my restless nature grew
till I cursed the arc which suckled me
with claustrophobic rue

Beyond the casing of the cradle
beyond the arc's curved arms
the sea called to my safe-sick soul
with all her worldly charms

And I cried back to G-d and fate
like Jonah from the fish
a prayer so frantic for escape
that G-d fulfilled my wish

And spit me out with open mouth
from within the whale cocoon
delivered me to churning sea

like one thrown from the womb

And suddenly my mouth was filled
with salt alien to my taste
while sights and sounds of curse surround
my fateful fall from grace

I tremble tread among the dead
beneath sky sore with rain
and faced with earth's reality
the flood became my pain

So terror seized I tore through sea
in search of semblance of ship
and found its curve beneath my feet
submerged to arc's round tip

Suspended calm and floating there
with just its top revealed
was island apexed synagogue
which waters dare not conceal

With weary want I climbed the curve
which once had arched my head
and from my mouth rained forth a song -
a prayer for all the dead

I peered into this hanging sphere
through the window of painted glass
and yearned for all that i had lost
in the sanctuary of my past

To be a bird caught in that cage
or to be an angel on high

I gazed as if into myself
and silently I cried

And at the apex of the roof
of their inverted ship
a window round of painted glass
let fall a single drip

.

MIRROR MOMENT:

Question #1: Remember back to the sanctuary of your youth. What memories stand out? Have you rebelled or embraced, ignored or transcended it?

Question #2: Imagine you are struck by that next drip. Do you have an *arc of comfort* in your life that you need to transcend?

_____

_____

_____

_____

_____

_____

_____

_____

_____

_____

_____

_____

_____

_____

_____

_____

_____

__

✦

CHAPTER 2

THE MYSTIC

My teenage rebelliousness was actually my first step from the Bible Belt to the Holy Land. Believe it or not folks, my lawlessness eventually led to a life filled with law—Jewish law. Whenever I see friends of mine from high school they are shocked that I, reckless & rebellious Cary Kaplan, am now an Orthodox Jews, married to an Orthodox Rabbi, living in Jerusalem.

*

CINDY

"Cary Kaplan, is that YOU?" shrieked Cindy as she caught a glimpse of me in the bathroom mirror. *"Good Lord, girl, what did you do with your hair? I'm sweatin' like a hooker in church and you got three scarves round your head!"*

"What, you're religious? You're livin' in Jerusalem? Oh, so you're sorta like a Jewish nun?"

"Oh, so you're not a nun. I see, so you **do** *have relations? Yeah, I heard about that sheet with the hole in it…"*

"That's an urban legend you say. Well, thank G!d for that."

"So you're more like a born-again Jew? Well, you know, my cousin, Chrisy, she's a born again. That's right. You know, she was a lot like you. She was a big cheerleader too. She says she's now a cheerleader for God. She's even got this cheer her and her friends do, 'Pray with us, you gotta gotta gotta pray with us…Ha-lay-lu-ya!'"

"Do y'all do cheer-leading for God over there in Jerusalem? No? Well, you can borrow that one….I will say, Cary Kaplan, you are the last person I would ever imagine goin' religious. I mean, you were as wild as a hyena in heat, a skunk in a perfume shop. I mean, you were handlin' more drugs than a Wallgreens in the wintertime girl! I am in shock!"

Well, Kaya, bless your heart. I know you're in danger over there. We pray for you at my church. Well, I gotta go; I'm fixin' to go down to Walmart. Y'all stay safe over there, a'right?!"

I try to tell my Memphis friends —"Yall, you don't get it. The impulse that moved me to shop-lifting and drugs was the same drive that, in the end, led me to God. It was just a desire for something alive, vital, meaningful."

My rebelliousness was like greasy fast food for a famished soul. It gave me a quick fix with a foul after-taste. Thankfully, by 17, I found a much healthier form of rebellion. I found the more wholesome fare of 'New Age Spirituality'. I became a Buddhist…or was it a Hindu…or maybe a Taoist? It's not entirely clear. All I know is that I went head-long into an authentic spiritual journey.

THE NEW AGE BOOKSTORE

At the New Age bookstore
crystals hangin' on the door
incense in the coffee shop
esoteric non-stop.

I-ching, The Artist's Way,
Kerouac, Earth Day
Kastenada, Emerson
slippin' hallucinogens.

Tibetan Book of the Dead
yoga with some dead-heads
neo-pagan reggae
give me suma that New Age cool-aid.

Ram Daas, 'Be Here Now'
philosophizin' bout the Dao
(though to talk about it's not the Dao
I'd schmooze about it anyhow).

Nostalgic for the 60's – why can't we all be hippies?
Astrology & tantra - no manicures, just mantras.
- Tarot cards? Read my rhunes!
Carl Jung, I'm gonna swoon!

Enlightenment, eternal bliss
I'm meditating, disciplined
Forget the shul, I'm goin Zen
Ashram, Ashram let me in!

MIRROR MOMENT:

What are the books that have most impacted your development?
List below the books that have been part of your spiritual journey.
What do they say about you and your path?

_____
_____
_____
_____
_____
_____
_____
_____
_____
_____
_____
_____
_____
_____
_____
_____
_____
_____
_____
_____
_____
_____
_____

KUNDALINI 101

Parody aside, all that discipline and focused breathing paid off. I became an avid meditator. And one exceptional night I was graced with my first and to this day unmatched, mystical experience.

It was night 79 of my alternate nostril breathing regimen. There I was, perched on my meditation cushion. Had on my favorite CD of Sri Lankan rainforest crickets. Flanked by my crystals and swimming in incense.

Close the right nostril, breathe in through the left, counting for four. Hold for eight. Out through the right, counting for four. In through the right, count for four. And out through left for eight...or was it hold for eight? No, IN for eight...out for four. And which nostril was I on?! Oy! Enough with this! This stuff is just way too complex for my Jewish nostrils!

I decided to just turn over and go to sleep. When suddenly a gust of energy rushed in through my toes. A tidal wave of Kundalini energy swirled up my spine and drenched me in a satori of body-transcending spiritual ecstasy! Red swirling light, euphoria, peace, enlightenment. It was classic Kundalini awakening 101 and I was One-Oh-One with All!

In that moment of mysterium tremendum, I experienced oneness, plain and simple. I would later learn that this was a text book mystical experience down to the detail. I had been touched, called, held, by some indescribable God-force. God-force. And certainly not a Jewish God—this had nothing to do with Judaism. This was simply and universally the Divine lacing that graces all of our lives, no matter our culture or creed.

My spiritual journey was like a rocket that had blasted off and was propelled into space. I had broken through, no longer land-locked to details or specifics like name or religion. In the wash of ultimate oneness there was no me, certainly no Jewish me. My spiritual journey was universal.

And yet, inevitably, life's natural gravity would call my rocket back down to the ground...to find myself a home. And for me, that house was destined to have a mezuza at the door.

For, in addition to its adventures in shop-lifting, my Hebrew school days had made one other lasting impression. And that was the Holocaust.

SHOAH BUSINESS

I LOVED the Holocaust! I know it's weird but the *only* thing about Judaism that was even remotely interesting to me was the torture of my ancestors.

So I jumped when I heard about this program called the "The March of the Living." A journey for high-schoolers to travel through the concentration camps of Poland—ending up with a grand finale visit to Israel to celebrate Israeli Independence Day.

I remember applying for a spot and having my interview, sitting across the table from the director of BBYO. In a suit, yet strangely effeminate...

THE INTERVIEW

*"Now, Cary, we've read over your application. Lovely job," he added, giving me the thumbs up. "It seems you really **love** the Holocaust. Though we call it the Shoah, around here. And you know what they say, 'There's no business like Shoah business!'"*

"But, seriously, I hate to break the news to you. But we did a little investigative research. We talked to some of your peers, and it appears that your peers (pun intended!)...well, they say that you're a party girl."

"You know, concentration camps and parties—just not a fit. They clash, like Barbara Streisand trying to rap, you know. We're sorry. We're not going to be able to let you into the program."

In that moment I was willing to forgo every wine-cooler-shlugging boy-kissing lipstick-swiping opportunity that my future might hold if they would but let me go on this trip. I jumped in quick defense:

"Nooo, I'm not a party girl; that was so Sophomore year! Now I'm a Junior—and a mystic. Lemme tell you about this mystical experience I had—Sri Lankan crickets—ecstatic Kundalini energy in through my toes...."

Sure enough, they let me in. And sure enough, this trip split me open. I wept my way through Eastern Europe. I wrote reams of second-rate Holocaust poetry, took macabre black and white photos of train tracks. Kissed the ground when we stepped off the plane in Tel Aviv.

It was an absolute paradigm shift. The paradigm shift had hit the fan. I suddenly actually wanted to be a Jew.

My gateway into Judaism was the gruesome past of my people. Now I wish I could say that I got turned-on to Judaism because of some joyful Shabbat song or a bite of a really finely done potato-kugel; but it wasn't. The thing that first pulled me in was images of my emaciated tortured ancestors and my sense of responsibility towards them. It was so not the comfortable numbness of my childhood, nor was it the detached bliss of my Buddhist practice. It was the heart-wrenching pain of my people. My doorway came through shared mourning, that thick super-glue of shared grief.

At Auschwitz my rocket fell out of the universal stratosphere and straight into this little cozy Jewish house. A house where I had siblings, lots of them —and we shared a history...and we shared a language. And the babble of my upbringing got a little more coherent.

For when we share mourning, we share housing.

In shared grief we become family.

THE PITTANCE OF ADMISSION

This House of Israel is in mourning.
We sit upon the floor and weep
the mirrors are black,
our robes are slashed,
and leather-less our feet.

Our clan is clad in ash and sack
a dirge between our bones
a wail of anguish unabated
rises from this home.

The pittance of admission here
is expression of lament
—authentic, rasp and risen
mangled and intense.

Here the graves are multiple
and flanked with stacking stones
which could, perhaps, be launched at enemies
but sit instead in memory of what is gone.

Our weaponry is our weeping;
our protection is our prayer
our strength is born when we gather to mourn
made siblings by shared despair.

And in lamentation lies our comfort
and in this meeting, our home is built
founded firm on the raw resilience
of the families of the killed.

But hear this, our love is

mightier than our anger!
For we are a nation of mothers
and fathers and priests.

We build houses out of war-stones
and change cemeteries into sanctuaries
with our songs of hope.

A knock upon the lintel lets in the shiva guests.
God shuffles in amongst them
and bends to offer His condolences.

And in the madness of the mourning
and the anguish so immense
a dwelling is suddenly erected
- regal & resplendent.

And a sacred space is made
amidst the family who endures
such loss and grief.

And our homeland looms strong
amidst the weeping throng
and God's Presence refuses to leave.

MIRROR MOMENT:

Question #1: How do you turn cemetaries into sanctuaries?

Question #2: Who do you mourn?
Who are you when you mourn?

_____

_____

_____

_____

_____

_____

_____

_____

_____

_____

_____

_____

_____

_____

_____

_____

_____

_____

_____

_____

_____

_____

_____

_____

CHAPTER 3

JERUSALEM FEVER

(THE SHMALTZ HITS THE FAN)

So I came back to Israel the very next chance I got. The summer after I graduated high school—1993. I went to what I thought was the Israeli dream—to live on a kibbutz. I did lots of farming, lots of kibbutz-laundry and lots of drinking beer. Then we got a weekend off. All of my friends went off to the beach in Tel Aviv to party. But the mystic in me whispered, "Jerusalem."

I jumped on the Egged express and as if I had a magnet in my backpack, headed straight to the Western Wall.

*

RABBI SHUSTER

There I was wandering around dreamy-eyed at the Western Wall plaza when I caught the attention of one Rabbi Meyer Shuster, God bless him. An awkward, lanky, holy, gangsta for God. He approached me as if he was a drug-dealer and in this sort of hunched-over mysterious style, said, 'Nu, where are you for Shabbas?"

I didn't even know what he was saying. It was like he was speaking a different language. I looked at him blankly.

He repeated emphatically, 'Nu, where are you for Shabbas?"

"Nowhere, where should I be?"

He peered into my eyes and said, "YOU, you should be in Shabbas!"

He proceeded to escort me up to the Heritage House—a life-changing little Old City outreach establishment with a standing offer of a free bed, free meals and free Torah classes.

And thus transpired the first full-on, law-keeping, mind-blowing Shabbat of my life. Rabbi Shushter was right; I needed to be 'in shabbas.' I prayed at the Western Wall. I went to a magical Friday night meal with a Hassidic family in Mei Shaarim.

I was floating in a Chagall painting where angel-faced people sat around ornate tables and sang, and actually talked—out loud—about God and spiritual experiences. This time it was the schmaltz that hit the fan. I was knee-deep in Shabbas schmaltz and loving in!

No one in Memphis Tennessee ever sat around and sang, and certainly no one ever talked about G-d or mystical experiences. I was in my element. I wanted more of this religious stuff and Rabbi Shuster was all too happy to escort me to it. Sunday morning he shows up bright & early at the Heritage House.

"Here's 50 shekels," he said waving the bill in his hand, "You jump into this cab and tell them 'Take me to Neve Yerushalayim – write this down! – Neveeeee Yerushalaaaayim Seminary. Tell him, 'Take me to learn some Torah!!'"

And that's exactly what I did. I was the Jewish Outreach Rabbi's dream girl—totally open, spiritual, impressionable. Suddenly I was learning Torah, mind-boggling, soul-expanding Torah. And I was not alone.

There was a whole rag-tag band of us -

American stow-away souls

with dread locks and mohawks,

with yoga mats and cowboy hats,

with discreet tattoos and nothing to lose,

ready to up and lift the top off of our hither-to existence

to erupt onto the streets of Yerushalayim!

High as an l'chaim!

Totally turned on by Torah.

THE RETURN

So this is what it means to be a Jew,
Who knew?! Who knew?!

That Judaism was ancient
and yet progressive.
mystical, intellectual
and impressive.

Grounded yet elevating
paradoxical and penetrating.

Suddenly I am plumbing depths
and thumbing through texts
that have been thumbed and plumbed
for generations past
and more to come.

Living the return of
Judah's long lost children
so far gone, so far hidden
now come home to the old books
of our own venerable tradition.

And so we pace ourselves
with the stealth
of a leopard
on the chase of the truth
which darts like a gazelle
through these hills of Yehuda
and tomes of Gemara
we will come to know so well.

With a fire hotter

than a 1000 degrees
from the cool Ivy League

OUR ivy climbs the Western Wall
- a beanstalk tall to which we cleave.

Finally, we have returned
to have our turn
on these ancestral streets

We are a prayer answered
after a 2000 year petition.
We are the limbs
Living out the prophet's vision.

And we ex-Patriot Jewish mystics were not alone in this ecstatic sense of arrival. There were pilgrims pouring in from every corner of the globe. From every religion, every division...all united & ignited & by the high that is Yerushalayim in the summertime!

Like a moveable feast of pilgrim's feet, one moving afternoon, I witnessed the Parade of the Nations take over Jerusalem's streets. Tens of thousands of devout Christians from across the planet, marching with flags and prayers, gifts and cheers, dancing, gleaming, singing, "Pray for the peace of Jerusalem."

Now these were pilgrims! I mean, the only pilgrims I had ever seen were at Thanksgiving school plays. But these were real live hard-core pilgrims hitting the pavement with a raucous and an honest to G!d adoration of the land of Israel! I was enthralled.

There we all were together - caught up in the thrill of living **in our very limbs** the fulfillment of prophets' visions of return to the land of Israel. When the exiles will be ingathered and the nations will clamor to come in honor of the holy wonder that is Jerusalem. It was nothing less than a historical miracle happening before our eyes!

CALLING ALL

Calling all pilgrims to come
to these courtyards of Jerusalem.

Come seeking wisdom
and higher vision
Be done beating drums
of conflict & division.

Come in streaming
like four cornered gleanings
clamoring with higher calling
cleaving to deeper meaning
shining with persistence
and a 3000 year-old commitment.

Commitment to the Spirit,
to the Bible, to the Torah
to something more than
the mores & norms
of the Western world
with her hordes of the
immoral and the impure.

Committed to something more
than a Manhattan latte
and a pumped-up paycheck
to "provide for the family"
that may smile wide
for the cameras
but weeps inside for their
bankrupt neshamas[3].

---

[3]Neshama means 'soul' in Hebrew.

Famished for a richer truth
than the loose change of material gain.
Famished for the fresh fruit of the Live Tree
- of Jerusalem with leaves of flame!

So fellow pilgrims of peace
Come stride these streets with me
Breathe these books
and dream these dreams with me.

For Jerusalem is a tree of life
*that has the strength to **change our lives***
If we but sit amongst her leaves and dream.

So come and eat and sing
Amongst Jerusalem's leaves
and dream…

MIRROR MOMENT:

Question 1: In what ways have Jerusalem changed or impacted your life?

Question 2: Have you ever been a pilgrim? What do you make *your* pilgrimage to?

_____
_____
_____
_____
_____
_____
_____
_____
_____
_____
_____
_____
_____
_____
_____
_____
_____
_____
_____
_____
_____
_____
_____
_____

CALLING THE PARENTS

There's a psychological disorder called "the Jerusalem Syndrome". It refers to any religiously themed obsessive ideas, delusions or psychosis....all of which are triggered by a visit to Jerusalem. It's been called "Jerusalem squabble poison," or "fievre Jerusalemmiene". (That's French for the Jerusalem fever! You know, that funky 70's dance move....do a shukkle, shukkle and a bow!)

On average, 100 tourists come into Jerusalem's hospitals annually suffering from this disorder. I think I might have had a small case of it, but it was far from *suffering*, I was thoroughly enjoying it.

My parents, on the other hand, were not quite so enamored with my fievre Jerusalemmiene. They're just not the feverish type.

I remember calling them to tell them the very exciting news about how I had become religious...and taken on a Hebrew name.

"Mom and Dad, hi, it's Cary. Actually, it's – CHAYA!"

"That's right,, I've decided to change my name."

"No, no, nothing's wrong with Cary. I just want to express my Jewish roots."

"No, not Chia, Mom—Chaya."

"Not Kaya—just drop the c—Haya."

"No, they didn't give me the name at the kibbutz. I left the kibbutz. It just wasn't where it's at. I'm in Jerusalem; I'm learning Torah. I'm going to these classes and doing Shabbas and eating with these amazing Orthodox families."(listens)

..."I don't know, like ten, twelve kids." (listens)

..."No, I don't know what these people do for a living, but they're amazing families. Yeah, I mean—" (listens)

"—A CULT? No Ma!"

"Well, yes, maybe. I guess you could say it's a little bit like a cult. But Mom, it's our cult! Yours, too!"

"Oh, my G-d, you guys should come! You've got to come and learn Torah—"(listens)

"—Return ticket? NO, Dad, I haven't set my return ticket yet....I understand YOU think I should come home. I just don't know if I really am ready to go to college, Dad."

THE C BOMB

And that was it; I had dropped the C bomb— *Not go to **College**.* It was my parents' worst nightmare. Because you must understand, if there was one thing my entire upbringing had been preparing me for, it was not going to live like a penniless mystic in Jerusalem. It was going to college. For my parents, the 11th commandment was: *Thou shalt send thy child to an Ivy League University.* Once I dropped the college bomb, that was the end of it; my parents brought out the big guns.

"What do you mean—not go to college?" Mom sobbed. "What kind of a life will you lead if you don't go to college? You'll end up in poverty with twelve shmaltzy children with names we can't pronounce."—and on and on and on.

Sure enough, two weeks later I was on the plane to be back in America in time for fall semester at my tidy Ivy League University. And to my parents' credit, I would do the *exact same* thing now if I was in their shoes. But at the time, in the heat of my fievre Jerusalmienne, well, it was a total bummer for my fervor.

On the plane home I passionately scribbled out this poem:

VELVET PEBBLE

I am a velvet pebble
in the palm of G-d's great hand.

For He stands upon the shoreline
of this lake called Holy Land.
And He skips the velvet pebbles
which He picks up from the sand.

Each pebble has its parable
each plans its own life span.
How many skips until it dips
to never skip again?

When will my velvet pebble
finally feel that weight of fate?
How many skipping dripping trips
to Israel will it take?

As sure as the twist of God's great wrist
determines each twist of fate,
as sure as a rock meets gravity
—I'll plunge into that lake.

MIRROR MOMENT:

Question 1: Is there any way that you feel like a velvet pebble being skipped? What is some destination or goal that you dip into but then skip back out of again?

Question 2: Have you dipped into the waters of Israel? The pebble in the poem is velvet so that it can absorb the water. What did you absorb from your trip that you carry with you?

_____
_____
_____
_____
_____
_____
_____
_____
_____
_____
_____
_____
_____
_____
_____
_____
_____
_____
_____
_____
_____
_____

_____
_____
_____
_____
_____
_____
_____
_____
_____
_____
_____
_____
_____
_____
_____
_____
_____
_____
_____
_____
_____
_____
_____
_____
_____
_____

_____

◇

CHAPTER 4

ALIYAH

& YERIDAH[4]

In college I took whatever spiritual fixes I could get, majored in Religious & Jewish Studies...though it was far from the juicy mystic that moved me the way that Jerusalem had. So, as soon as I graduated – I plunged again. This time to make *aliyah*.

There's a famous Biblical verse about God taking the Hebrews out of Egypt to the Promised Land, "I bore you on the wings of eagles and brought you to me." Beautiful, right? Born up majestic on eagles' wings, the wind blowing through our hair, divinely-purchased first class tickets!

Well, the Israeli poet Chaim Bialik once said, "Reading the Bible in translation is like kissing a woman through a veil." So, with this particular quote, it's like lifting the veil to find that you were kissing your creepy Math teacher. Because the Hebrew word used for eagle – *nesher* - actually, isn't a regal eagle at all. It is rather – a vulture. And boarding onto a carcass-eating scavenger's wing just doesn't have that same sort of first-class ring.

---

[4]*Aliyah* literally means 'to ascend'. It is the Hebrew term used for the process of moving to live in Israel. The word *yerida* on the other hand, means 'to go down' and is used to refer to leaving Israel.

Little did I know but I was about to meet my vulture. For, shortly after I arrived in Israel….so did the Intifada[5]. Bombed buses and exploding cafes. Armies worth of people unabashedly promising to decimate my dream-state. Suddenly – and inevitably - I was faced with the babble of the battle-ground. And the need to determine where-oh-where did I stand in relation to that beast known as the conflict in the Middle East.

In my 15 years of living in Israel, I have lived in three different cities: Jerusalem, Yafo (Jaffa) and Bat Ayin. Now, you have to understand, Yafo and Bat Ayin are about as opposite as you can get on the political spectrum.

Yafo is a beach-front Arab alcove attached to Tel Aviv. Left wing to the extreme. Bat Ayin is a small, radical Jewish settlement in the West Bank, right wing extreme. I felt both comfortable and at times highly uncomfortable, in both. I'm less left or right wing, and more 'in-between' wing. *Inbetwing*, if you will. After all, you need two wings to fly.

So first we start in Yafo. You must understand, Yaffo is basically 30% Muslim, 30% Arab Christian, 30% Jewish, 10% goat. I *kid you not*, I would wake up to find goats sleeping on the roof of my car. I felt like I was making private peace treaties on a daily basis, at the corner store, on the sidewalks, at the cafes.

---

[5]Palestinian uprising.

My street, Kedem, right on the beach, was famous for its Arab fish restaurants that weekly got converted into wedding halls for these massive Arab weddings. Men in one fish restaurant. Women in the restaurant next door. How's that for a *mechitza*[6]?

One night, I got up the hutzpa to pop my head into the 'women's restaurant.' To my delight, I noticed all my neighbors were there! Ibtisam was the first to notice me. Ibtisam, the 300–pound-Muslim mama of the neighborhood, bounded over to me. She was like a mix between Yasser Arafat, Borat and your classic *yiddishe mama*.

IBTISAM

"Ahlan, Chaya, habibi," Ibtisam hooted. "Come, you must dance with the bride! She will be so happy to see your American face."

"Come, I will show you what an Aaaarab wedding is like. This is how we dance for the bride. First the bride is in the middle and we dance in circles around her. Very unique Arab dance. We call it circle dancing."

"We make her happy. You go. You clap, you shake. You must go and make the bride happy, now, Go. You dance, you shake. Smile. Show her your big white American teeth. In sh'allah soon by you, Chaya. Hamdalila!"

Ibtisam had spoken. I obeyed.

As I joined in the circle I realized, "Oh, Lord, this is exactly like a Jewish wedding! The circle dancing, making the bride happy. This is

[6]A mechitza is a divider used in Orthodox Judaism to separate between the men and women in a religious setting.

closer to a traditional Jewish wedding than most of the Jewish weddings I've been to. Wow, we really are related! My cousins! I love my neighbors so much! I love Arabs! There IS peace in the Middle East!"

My inner peace activist was activated. I was making peace in the Middle East on Kedem Street!

Two ecstatic hours later: "Good-bye, Shokran. Thank you. Aywah. Mazal tov!" I stepped out onto Kedem, late night now in Jaffa. In the sudden quiet, it was just me and the pavement as I headed home.

Until I start to notice that it's not just me and the pavement after all. There's someone walking behind me. I look back. Oh, G-d, it's an Arab man, close behind me and getting closer. My heart is beating like that darbuka at the wedding.

"Remember, he's your cousin. He's probably just...escorting you. Remember, you just made peace in the Middle East. This guy is family..."

Within a minute, I shamelessly broke out into a sprint and didn't look back and didn't take a breath until I was on the other side of my locked door.

Scared, yet exhilarated, confused, yet inspired. I mean, are they my enemies, my cousins, my friends, my foes?

I realized that I was living the conundrum of the complexity that is Israel. It's easy to live in a place of clearly defined either/ors. Either your neighbors are your friends and you love them/tolerate them, or your neighbors are your enemies and you hate them/fear them/kill them. You certainly don't crash their weddings. In Israel, our neighbors are both. We live in the paradox, the grey, the *inbetwing.*

Suddenly a wash of pride overcame me. What an amazing opportunity this is, to cultivate a mighty moral discernment! To live in a land where enemy and neighbor are enmeshed. I'm not an Orthodox Jew; I'm a paradox Jew! I was walking in the midst of what I could only call the moral greatness known as living in the greyness.

THE INBETWING

Here we all grapple with the justice
of how to treat an 'enemy'.
When just next door she sleeps so peaceful
With prayers and knives...in kitchen sinks.

No black and whites, no rigid creed
but shared street lights and democratic
with equal rights and liberties.

Here we wrangle with the knowledge
That enemy is more than beast
More than faceless; more than target
Less of Other, More of Me.

And in this challenge will be our greatness
And in this challenge will be God's Name
That we two peoples pursuing justice
have thus been tested and proved humane.

Please G!d may we be proved humane.

MIRROR MOMENT

One of the hallmarks of the spiritual journey is the encounter with paradox. What paradoxes do you hold in your life? How do you live in the *inbetwing*?

_____

_____

_____

_____

_____

_____

_____

_____

_____

_____

_____

_____

_____

_____

_____

_____

_____

_____

_____

_____

_____

✧

BAT AYIN

And then there's the other side of the political spectrum. Within a few years I would find myself living in Bat Ayin; a religious settlement in the wild, wild, West Bank.

You see, I married Hillel. He's this wonderful California boy who decided to leave behind his cushy American career to come to Israel to become an Orthodox Rabbi. This in a country where Orthodox rabbis are as plentiful as rednecks in the deep South. (Or, as my relatives would say, "A Rabbi? That's no job for a nice Jewish boy!")

Of course he wanted the very highest spiritual training possible. Which just happened to be at this yeshiva[7] in the little bitty West Bank town of Bat Ayin. (Population 1000, with about 100 families. Yes, that's an average of 8 kids per family!)

Although we didn't agree with the politics of its more hard-core right-wing members, we loved the yeshiva, the rustic setting, the deep devotion and decency of the inhabitants...Oh, and the wildly affordable rent.

So, there I was, seven months pregnant with twins and living in a rickety trailer home on the side of a dank hill surrounded by hostile Arab villages. We were woken in the middle of the night to the shrill of sirens. I peered out the window to see a small army of Israeli soldiers, with guns cocked, swarming our small street.

---

[7]School for studying Torah. Often on the path towards becoming a Rabbi.

Hillel called the local security to hear the unraveling of the tragic tale. He was reluctant to tell me the details given that I was already in the midst of a hormone-crazed pregnancy. I gripped my belly and hissed insistently, "Hillel I can handle this. I can handle this!"

The details spilled out. Erez Levanon, a sweet-as-honey singer, songwriter and father of three had gone down into the valley, as he did daily, to meditate and pray. He was stabbed to death by two men from the neighboring Arab village. The soldiers found his body just down the hill from our caravan. It was like living in a horror movie.

That night we decided to move – with alacrity - from our hillside. I reassured my frantic parents on the phone, "Don't worry, we'll move to the center of town, the safest area of town possible!"

And so we got a nice place right there overlooking Bat Ayin's center square of town. Safe at last. Babies were born. Life glided along serenely. Until an otherwise peaceful afternoon, when an Arab man broke into town, sprinting down main street, brandishing a pick ax and headed straight for the town square.

When he got there, he found a small group of children playing by the post-office. Straight out a horror movie, he planted a nearly-fatal blow to the skull of a 7 year old. He then moved on to attacking a 5-year-old. A 5-year-old. He chased this small child with raised ax and crazed eyes. Luckily for the 5-year-old, there was a heroic 13-year-old also fatefully at the post-office that day.

Shlomo Nativ, our next-door neighbor. Shlomo was slaughtered while protecting this 5-year-old child. 13-year-old tragic hero, Shlomo Nativ, with his long blond payes[8] and clear as sky blue

---

[8] Payes – or payot – are the side-curls worn by many Orthodox men and boys.

eyes…killed out my kitchen window in the center of town on an otherwise peaceful afternoon. And once again…a wail of anguish was raised in the house of Israel…

This House of Israel is in mourning.
We sit upon the floor and weep.
The mirrors are black, our robes are slashed,
and leather-less our feet.

Our clan is clad in ash and sack
—a dirge between our bones.
A wail of anguish—unabated
rises from this home.

But unlike with the Holocaust, this time the mourning didn't leave me feeling cozy and connected in a little Jewish cottage. This mourning left me isolated, broken — bereft of connection, bereft of comfort. What was the moral greatness I was supposed to find in all of this?

I was a wreck. I turned to Hillel weeping, "I can't handle this. I CAN'T handle this." I was done with the paradox and complexity. I was done with the incessant badgering call to moral greatness. I was not made for martyrdom or witnessing martyrdom. I was made for the first flight back to Memphis, Tennessee.

We headed back to the Bible Belt, the babble belt. But this time I was the one who was babbling. I felt like the personification of Babel's toppled tower—tongue-twisted, crumbled in confusion. Sitting on the plane as my velvet pebble skipped again, this is what I wrote:

BABEL'S DAUGHTER

I am Babel's daughter
once a builder
now bewildered
as my tower crumbles
into but a rubble
of incoherence and regret.

Where once stood a stacking shrine of promise
now lay a shattered pack of fallen bricks.

And my world was suddenly
more messed up than mystic
more full of holes than holy
more bad deal than ideal.

I have lost my language
somewhere amidst a foreign slang.
All that was once sensible
now reprehensible
and strange.
My mother tongue now mangled
Babel's daughter is my name.

MIRROR MOMENT:

Question #1: What is your broken Tower of Babel, some ideal structure you had built that ended up in shambles?

Question #2: What is 1 thing that most confuses or disturbs you about Israel. And how do you hold those challenging parts of your relationship with Israel?

_____

_____

_____

_____

_____

_____

_____

_____

_____

_____

_____

_____

_____

_____

_____

_____

_____

_____

_____

_____

_____

_____
_____
_____
_____
_____
_____
_____
_____
_____
_____
_____
_____
_____
_____
_____
_____
_____
_____
_____
_____
_____
_____

CHAPTER 5

THE INTEGRATION

The tower of my ideal spiritual Israel, land of prophecies come true, was shattered by soldiers' boots and bloodshed. But maybe the crumbling of my towering ideal was a good thing. For it allowed me to greet a more eye-level reality.

Sitting there in all that rubble of a too-tall-tower-built, I realized that I needed to straighten myself out. Was I a peace activist or a martyr or a Jewish American princess who had foolishly fled her castle...

What was *my* truth? Was it everything that the rabbis told me? Or everything that the media told me? Or how about those lovely ideals of my American friends and family?

I was a psychotherapist after all, I preached daily about the importance of following your own voice. – I decided to start following my own advice and began the tough work of excavating my innards. There, in the midst of all that rubble, I got to know myself, not just the voices of parents or teachers, rebels or Rabbis...shredded all the sound bites and took the time to listen to my own silence instead.

Sifting through my tower's debris, I took another long look

at my childhood—that place I had been so busy rebelling against for so many years. I realized it really wasn't an "arc of comfort" at all. I realized it was actually more like a *bayit ne'eman* - a reliable house.

Now you have to understand what I mean by a reliable house. When a Jewish couple gets married the traditional blessing people say to them is, "You should be blessed to build a *bayit neeman b'yisrael.*" *Bayit* means home and *ne'eman* means faithful, secure, reliable. *You should build a reliable house in Israel.* (best said with thick New York accent.)

A reliable house is just about the opposite of a Tower of Babel...that kind of over-stretched structure that is made to crumble. The tower of my ideal Israel might have been high-reaching & impressive, but it was destined for doom.

After all was said and done, I realized that what I deeply wanted was to build a reliable house where my children could strive and thrive and fall and feel well-held through it all.

I finally understood that that was the great inheritance that my parents had gifted me. Okay, it was in Memphis Tennessee. But it was *reliable.* And I finally realized what an immeasurable gift it was.

With this reframe, I came to see that there are really 2 types of holy lands – an inner and an outer. One's an Israel of latitude...and one of attitude. A holy land of attitude is where Israel is a *universal* metaphor, a state of mind, an inner-terrain. This is the universal holy land...to which every person must make their own pilgrimage in their own way.

And then there's the holy land of latitude...and longitude. It's that actual place on a map. A parliamentary democracy on the south-east shore of the Mediterranean Sea. Some seven and a half million people big, 290 miles long, the singular homeland of the Jewish people…as well as home to lots of other peoples too.

Israel is at once an objective sovereign state, as well as a subjective state of mind. So why was it that it was so hard for me to maintain my *inner Israel attitude* when I was in the actual Israel latitudes?

It was clear to me that being wrecked by grief while living in the State of Israel was a betrayal of my inner state of Israel. Maybe I just needed to focus on building a bayit neeman amongst the multitude of other lovely and reliable homes I was surrounded by in America?

THE VISION

I was confused. I needed guidance, direction. That's when I discovered this powerful ritual that I started doing every few days. It entailed a type of soul journey...*to Target...with my mother's credit card.* The ritual crescendoed with a sacramental mocha-chino grandee at Starbucks. It was a deeply transformative spiritual practice!

And it worked. Because one afternoon, as I sat there in caffeinated bliss, reading a book, I came across the following story:

Before the establishment of the modern Israel, the UN offered David Ben Gurion a Partition Plan. This plan would have left the Jewish people with a paltry slice of territory—but it would nevertheless have been the realization of a Jewish homeland!

Ben Gurion could not decide, and so called forth his trusted colleague, Yitzhak Tabenkin, to help him make the decision. Tabenkin asked for a day in which to consider his response. He said, "You must give me a day. I need to consult with two individuals."

The next day, Tabenkin returns and urges Ben Gurion to refuse the offer. Ben Gurion listens, ponders, nods and replies, "I agree with your decision, but tell me, from whom did you seek advice?"

"From two people," answered Tabenkin. "From my grandfather and from my grandson. From my grand-father who died ten years ago, and from my grandson who is not yet born."

Something about the rush of the caffeine and sugar mixed with this great story was magical for me. Because right there in the buzz of that crowded Starbucks, I sat down, closed my eyes, and went inside. Suddenly, I was back on that meditation cushion from high school, overtaken by a vision. I closed my eyes and saw myself surrounded by my ancestors and my descendants.

I was in a dark cave, surrounded by a host of shadowy figures who had gathered to discuss my destiny. The first one to step forward was my old yiddishe gramma, Mutsi Uditsky (with a name straight out of a Polish joke). She ambled over to me, pinched my cheeks real hard and said, "Zeeskeit, just be where you'll be happy—in here." As she pointed to my heart.

And then, out of the shadows stepped forward my luminescent future granddaughter, age 12, with a shining long braid. She approached me gently and in flawless Hebrew whispered, "*Anachnu babayit*"—We're home. We're home.

And then suddenly there came a whole countless chorus of Eastern European Edelsons, all my mother's kin from Tukum Latvia, the ones who suddenly stopped sending letters in 1943. They were all there, ghostly and silent, yet insistent.

And finally my great-grandson dressed as a soldier, who put his strong hand on my shoulder, his head to my cheek, and murmured, "You're safe." I'm safe.

By this point the sounds of Starbucks had thoroughly faded away. A memory came rushing up to the surface. It was me at age 8, JCC summer camp. There I was standing sturdy in shorts and t-shirt, at the flagpole for the morning raising of the flags. I watched in wonder as these two colorful cloths were hoisted to sky—an American and an Israeli flag, like the two parts of me.

And I, I was this little precious precocious pitskila, singing Hatikva[9] with all my heart, and my heart was like a tiger, fierce and clear and strong.

This young unabashed prophetess, little me, squeezing her eyes shut and singing beneath the flags.

This child, remarkably, was already sold on coming home to the Land of Israel. She was already there in the thick Bible Belt heat, belting out Hatikva at the top of her lungs. She was already there, even before the whole story unfolded, of swiped lipsticks and Auschwitz, well before that wondrous first glimpse of the Western Wall. She was already there, with Yerushalayim welling up overwhelming in her heart.

And she—she didn't know from fear. Didn't know how the path would unfold beneath her. She just knew her destination and her destiny.

And sitting there in Starbucks, wrapped up in this vision, all the waves of meaning, of history, of ancestry, washed over me. Like I was standing on the other side of the Sea of Reeds. Watching as all of those mighty chariots that had so crippled me with foreboding…simply got washed away. Washed away in this precious long-awaited drench of meeting myself, my ancestors, and my descendants.

---

[9]Hativka is the Israeli national-anthem.

MIRROR MOMENT:

Imagine, as you are sitting here, that your ancestors and your descendants are with you right now. Imagine they've been accompanying you all along. They have all gathered to discuss your spiritual path.

Who do you see? What do they say?

_____

_____

_____

_____

_____

_____

_____

_____

_____

_____

_____

_____

_____

_____

_____

_____

_____

_____

_____

_____

_____

_____

For me this vision clarified things. Suddenly, there was a sort of peace in the Middle East. For I had made MY peace with the conflict in the Middle East. I found my inner Israel attitude. Dwelt in my own inner reliability. Something I learned to do in my nice, secure American home. And from that secure place, some very deep, very old, part of me was incessantly singing Hatikva...yearning for Yerushalayim.

*

And so this time, with immense gratitude
I returned, not running from but running to.

I packed the best of the United States
into my suitcase...
to come to Israel to cultivate
a peaceful inner attitude in the
not-so-peaceful latitudes of the Middle East...

No longer rebelling but now rebuilding
the *bayit neeman* that my parent's had gifted me.

Because you can take the girl out of America
but you can't take America out of the girl.

And that's the secret y'all!
That's the gift of the Jewish people's
dispersion all around the world.

And with this

we reach our final twist
on the Tower of Babel.

For what was the babble all about?

*

Babel had a common culture
which built a breath-taking structure.

And then it was struck down into myriad tongues.
-    Does this national narrative sound familiar to anyone?

It's Jewish history wrapped in a metaphor!

We were once a united nation
with single tongue singing common song.
Until construction met destruction
And we were flung into dispersion.

Scattered to the four corners of the globe.
Mixed up and mingled with all that unknown.

Marinated in the sauce of loss….and of gain.
Simmering in assimilation
Babel's daughter is **all** of our names.

We've soaked in the spices
The virtues and vices
Of all the earth's cultures
And this synthesis is priceless.

And so we thread our tapestry
with seventy tongues worth of poetry.

With the spices of India,
the grit of America
The girth of Russia
the grace of Persia.

The abundance of the earth
Laid at our feet
To rebuild a rectified tower
piece by precious piece.

                              *

So if and when you go to the Western Wall,
OWN it, for it's your own.

You are an essential part
of the patchwork that is this home.

You have your own slice of the world
that is yours alone to bring.
Your own story of redemption
Your own incomparable song to sing.

And when you finish this book
—promise me one thing.

That you'll babble just a little bit more.
Be a little more confused
A little more Israel-infused.

Be a little more mixed up and a little more found
A little more connected to Israel's holy ground.

Be a child of Babel,
mixed up and found…
inextricably connected
to your *inner* holy ground…

MIRROR MOMENT:

What is your slice of the world that is yours and yours alone to bring. How do you contribute to the rebuilding of this Tower, this country? What do you bring?

_____

_____

_____

_____

_____

_____

_____

_____

_____

_____

_____

_____

_____

_____

_____

_____

_____

_____

_____

_____

_____

_____

MIRROR MOMENT #2

1. "What is your holy land?" Perhaps it is one of attitude, perhaps latitude, perhaps both?

2. What is the next step that you are called to take to reach *your* holy land? Take this opportunity to spell it out and & commit to it now.

_____
_____
_____
_____
_____
_____
_____
_____
_____
_____
_____
_____
_____
_____
_____
_____
_____
_____
_____
_____
_____

_____

_____

_____

_____

_____

_____

_____

_____

_____

_____

_____

_____

_____

_____

_____

_____

_____

_____

_____

_____

_____

_____

_____

FURTHER WRITINGS
& REFLECTIONS

Processing poem & questions for those who have visited Israel

WHAT REMAINS?

What remain of those Israel
adventures on bus and on plane ?

After all the revolutions of wheels
and rounds of meals
what are you still hungry for?

From Masada to mount of olives
what whispers of promise
did you harvest?

What mountain moved majestic in you?
How have you been deepened,
broadened, improved?

What spirit of the Western Wall
sticks to your bones?
What sloping scope of land
do you pack and take home?

What of all this will endure
after all of the stimulus is gone?
What passion will you pass on
to your children's generation
...and beyond?

How will you be a builder of Israel

Inner and outer
Attitude and latitude
Because both matter?

MIRROR MOMENT:
(for processing at the end of your Israel visit)

1. What "inner-souvenirs" do you take home with you from this trip? What moments most stand out & why? List 3 & explain.

_____

_____

_____

_____

_____

_____

_____

_____

_____

_____

_____

_____

_____

_____

_____

_____

_____

_____

_____

2. How does encountering the latitudes of Israel impact
   your *Israel of attitude*? List 3 ways & explain.

_____

_____

_____

_____

_____

_____

_____

_____

_____

_____

_____

_____

_____

_____

_____

_____

_____

_____

_____

_____

_____

_____

_____

3. How can you be a builder of Israel – inner & outer? Write out 5 ways below and commit to actually doing at least 1 of them.

_____

_____

_____

_____

_____

_____

_____

_____

_____

_____

_____

_____

_____

_____

_____

_____

_____

_____

_____

_____

_____

_____

_____

JERUSALEM

Jerusalem - Yerushalayim - means "Ir Shalom" - City of Peace. And yet, it has been destroyed twice, attacked 52 times, besieged 23 times, and captured and recaptured 44 times.[10] How can this city, so beleaguered by conflict, be named for peace? Is it irony or paradox, or perhaps something more?

It reminds me of another Biblical paradox – the burning bush. A symbol of the undoing of the natural order, where fire does not bring destruction...on the contrary, it brings revelation. The voice of God calls out from the impossible endurance of a shrub amidst flames.

That which should logically be destroyed, endures. And not just endures, but initiates and ushers in what is to become history's greatest symbol of liberation, the Exodus from Egypt. The fiery shrub is the holy ground from which God speaks.

This paradox of endurance amidst destruction is quite possibly one of the defining characteristics of the Jewish people. The State of Israel has been described as a phoenix, risen from the flames of the Holocaust.

But not only is it a country that has risen from the flames, it is a country that thrives amidst the flames of continuing fires of attack from her neighbors. It is a country ensconced in conflict, yet

---

[10]According to Eric H. Cline's tally in Jerusalem Besieged

somehow, at its best and highest, remains untouched.

And so too with Jerusalem. Never before has a metropolis weathered such unending quarrels. And yet, amidst the conflagration, she endures as a city of peace, issuing a message of godliness and the promise of salvation.

It is said that the burning bush was nothing extraordinary to most who looked upon it. A dozen others walked right past it. What proved Moses' greatness is that he saw the miracle within it. He turned aside and wondered at it. He heard God's voice in it. He removed his shoes.

Sometimes that is how I experience Jerusalem. Usually it is just the mundane domain where I shop and shlep my bags and pay my bills. But sometimes, at the best of times, I turn aside from the mundane drone of my day and see the astounding miracle that is being worked beneath my very feet.

The poem below is an invitation to stop and acknowledge the utter miracle of this city. An invitation to hear the voice of God issuing from each alley, each corner store, each traffic jam. May we, and the whole world, see Yerushalayim as a city which sits serene and enduring, offering peace, even amidst the flames.

THE BURNING BUSH

Jerusalem, my burning bush
A city so inflamed,
and yet, endurance is its name.

Here roam my heart & mind
Where, walk me soft,
and put my shoes aside

And let me admire more
this site
which burns
with no less bark
and no less branch
Eternal spark
within its stance

And blaze
My days with hers
And let no less than all of her endure

And may she brighter burn
that I may longer gaze and learn –
this mystery of Yours.

RACHEL'S PRAYER

(Poetic Commentary on Parshat Vayishlach)

Remember the Biblical love-at-first-sight story of Jacob meeting Rachel? Heroically, Jacob rolls the massive stone from atop the well to water her flock. Romantically, he precedes to kiss her and then lifts up his voice in weeping.

Though this is love at first sight, its consummation is vastly delayed. Jacob has to work 7 years for his deceptive Uncle Lavan before he is able to finally marry Rachel. A strenuous exercise in delayed gratification.

And yet, their love is so great that the text tells us that the 7 years were but a few days for Jacob. Because of this morphing of time he was able to withstand the waiting period. And his commitment becomes a model for a love that transcends time and space.

Indeed, this sense of time transcendence takes us back to the moment of Jacob's weeping at the well. For the Midrash shares that Jacob wept because he saw with prophetic foreknowledge that he and Rachel would not be buried together.[11]

In this week's Torah reading we see his premonition fulfilled. Rachel tragically dies in childbirth and is buried "along the road to Efrat" as opposed to in the family burial site. At that moment of the kiss, the bonds of time were transcended and he was able to have a prophetic vision of the future.

Granted, it is a painful vision. But it's not unlike the story of Rabbi Akiva who laughed when he beheld the tragic destruction of the

---

[11]Bereshit Rabbah 70:11

Second Temple.[12] He laughed because he realized that if the negative prophecy of destruction came true, then that would necessarily mean that all the positive prophecies of return and rebuilding would also come true for the Jewish people.

Indeed, we in our own days have had the enormous gift of witnessing the fulfillment, partial thought it may be, of the myriad prophecies of return to the Land of Israel.
We are the living recipients of that prophetic fruit.

In the poem below Rachel weeps for the fulfillment of the prophecy of her children's return to this land. She reminds us that just as Jacob love for her transcended time and allowed him to make it through those 7 years of work, so too if we beleaguered builders of Jerusalem can but access the vastness of our love for this land, then we can also weather through whatever waiting periods time may hold.

May we merit to witness the fulfillment of a true and enduring peace in this holy land.

---

[12] Talmud Makkot 24B

THE WAIT

You wept
As wet as wells
Having spilled
The crowning ton of stone
Onto the sand
With withered hands
but high romance

Made the skinny shepherds
call the place
- the wailing well -
for generations to come

And seven years
grown old
between your gaze and mine
- was like a day -
held between the gates
of withered hands
and weathered
wait

And know that
I weep as well
when memories of
the future spill
into our tent
and premonitions
limp into our
lamp-lit den

For if this ominous
prophecy
must be then promise me

to plant your stones
on that baneful road
where house my bones

And let memorial stand,
a somber marker
in a severed land

To mark the promise
of prophecy
of transcendence
of time and of distance
with a mother's mad insistence
that the exile of her children
must end

And when finally march
our children by
from their battered walk
through genocide
I will be weeping[13]
loud with pleading
at that corner-side
- where Jerusalem
meets Gush Etzion
with her border guards
and building zones

And I will lament with rage
the historic parade

---

[13] Foreseeing that the Jews on the way to exile would pass by the site, the Patriarch Jacob buried her on the road on the way to Ephrat and not within the city so that she would sense their anguish and pray for them (Bereishit Rabbah 82:10). Add to this the quote from Jeremiah, "A voice is heard in Ramah, lamentation, and bitter weeping, Rachel weeping for her children; she refuses to be comforted for her children, because they are not." (Jeremiah 31:15) Thus, Rachel stands as the archetype for the mother weeping for her children.

through Europe, Arabia
Aushchwitz, Asyria
and back to my grave
at Bethlehem's
barricades

And with the force of my weeping
and the form of your rocks[14]
will our children return
to the road to Efrat

And nineteen hundred years
- will be like a day -
held between the gates
of withered hands
and our children's
will to weather
the wait.

---

[14]It is interesting to note that Jacob in both of these stories is engaged in the moving of rocks. First he makes a stone altar (a matzava) at the site of his famous dream of the ladder. Then he moves the massive stone from atop the well for Rachel. And finally, in the story of her death, he again creates a matzeva, a stone memorial, upon Rachel's roadside grave.

COLLISION

Making Sense of the Violence
(Poetic Commentary on Parshat Vayeitze)

I wrote this piece during the Gaza conflict of 2012.
It is a commentary and poem on the weekly Torah reading and how it
corresponded with the events of the week.

I am *struck* by the fact that the Torah reading for this harrowing
week of conflict contains none other than the archetypal tale of
Jacob's ladder. The narrative opens with a powerful verb that
demands our attention. It reads, "*Vayifga* - Jacob
arrived/encountered the place."

This verb *yifga* carries with it a punch, quite literally. For much more
than mere arrival or encounter, *yifga* connotes a sense of collision –
of two objects striking each other. It is no mistake that this verb
shares its root with the modern Hebrew term for terrorist attack,
pegua, and for injured– *nifga*.

And hence the poignant parallel to this week, for this has after all
been a week of collisions, from the actual and awful exchange of
explosives, to the more subtle yet still-insidious throng of words
launched in the media and online.

This essential verb *yifga* colors our entire understanding of Jacob's
narrative and thus our own narrative…of our making sense of this
week, of this war, of the nature of the conflict that riddles this
Land.

For this is one of the Torah's defining stories of relationship with
the Land of Israel. First, "the place" that strikes Jacob is no less

than Mt. Moriah, the historic site of the binding of Isaac and of the Temple itself. And what's more, the core content of God's message to Jacob is nothing less than the promise that this land is given to his seed.

This vision is at once a mystic glimpse of the corridor connecting heaven and earth, as well as the highly political promise of Jewish possession of the Land of Israel.

As such, it is really no wonder that our current-day experience of "the place" is one so terribly fraught with violence, with awe and intensity. Just as Jacob collided with this spot, so too we do collide with this Land. Just as this was for Jacob the site of his father's fearful binding, and also a place of holiness and prayer, so too for so many of us, to be in Israel is to be struck, to be flooded, by both a sense of prayerfulness and fear.

Jacob wakes up after his astounding dream and exclaims, "God is in this place and I did not know it." He is filled with fear and adds, *'Mah nora hamakom hazeh'.* How awesome, how awful, is this place, the house of God..."

All too often we do not "know" that God is truly housed here. Certainly the evening news and trends of world-opinion would say the opposite. Even the uber-holy Jacob didn't get it! Even Jacob admits he did not apprehend G!d here. That is, not until he was hit by it. Not until that *pegua* of Mt. Moriah had thoroughly struck him into a state of knowing.

And so perhaps it is with us too. That with each hit, with each *pegua*, we can access some otherwise inaccessible revelation of the God. I admit that it is arguably absurd to ask or expect that anyone could, or should, behold God in these horrific attacks.

And yet, I must speak for myself and say that I find solace in this teaching. I find solace in the fact that it is *this* week that we learn about Jacob's fearsome collision with Mt. Moriah. I find solace in the fact that we have a long religious tradition of mixing prayer and Jerusalem and fear. The violence that accompanies Israel, as unfortunate as it may be, is but a testimony to the fact that this place is full of God, fearsomely full of God.

Yes, this week I could easily see myself as a victim of hateful attacks, or as a partaker in a national narrative of violence. *Or* I can stretch for significance in the face of all this violent absurdity. I can close my eyes and dream God into this place. I can envision the ladder connecting all this dross of worldliness to something so much higher.

Yes, this place is awesome. Yes, like Jacob, my voice cracks with fear. And yes, like Jacob, I utter an affirmation that God is here. Even with each fresh *pegua*, "God is here."

Collision

Count me as one who has
collided
with this mountain,
with this gravelly amalgam
of prayer and fear.

A place so revered
for 3-thousand years
that I have no choice
but to stop in my tracks
and pay homage
to the impact
of Moriah.

And though the truth
be hidden
in the conflict
and her spinning dust
yet I have glimpsed enough
to know that
this is none other than
the House of God.

And yes,
she is replete with
sonic booms
and safe rooms
where huddled children
howl as sirens sound
and war looms.

But still
this is our sacred ground.
Rattled and riddled
with bullets and shrapnel
with blood-let

and battle.

And yet
it is
ironically and eternally
unruffled
by the prattle
of our enemies.

This place is our very own concoction
of awful and awesome.
Of blessing and foreboding
All folded up
Beneath us
As we sleep upon
our rocky beds
and dream.

*

You, God, have granted us
the vision of prophets
at this collision spot
of pain & promise.

You have opened our eyes
to behold the ladder
lapping sky
that we might exclaim,
"God was here all along
And I, I did not know."

And so we find refuge
in this sacrament
of dirge and dirt.

And pray
at this monument
of faith

known as
"The Place"
where heaven
collides with earth.

A PISGAH PARABLE

FOR ISRAELI INDEPENDENCE DAY

At the finale of the Torah we read, "And Moses went up from the plains of Moab unto Mount Nebo, to the top of Pisgah…and the Lord showed him all the land…" (34:1) Pisgah was the specific name for a series of mountain ranges in the high plateau of Moab. Elsewhere these ranges are designated by the more general name, "Har hevarim", i.e. "the mountain of the regions beyond".

This appellation points to the fact that climbing Pisgah is essentially about going to the place where one passes on to the next region, the next phase, of one's journey. This climb is not necessarily about Moses' end, or even the Torah's end, but about seeing 'beyond', to the next step of the journey, for Moses and for Israel. The lesson of Pisgah is that of seeing into what lies beyond.

Likewise, Pisgah can be seen as the archetypal vantage point from which the Land of Israel is to be viewed. Surely then it can be instructive for how we today view the Land of Israel. Just look at one of the central images of Yom Ha'atzmaut, Israeli Independence-Day. Israelis take to the streets with clamoring celebration.

A central ritual of the holiday is to roam the streets toting little rubber hammers with which to hit one's fellow revelers. These hammers are really quite symbolic of one of Yom Haatmaut's most poignant themes. On the one hand we feel the joy of finally establishing a Jewish state; of finally reaching one of the long awaited apexes of Jewish history.

And yet, we are simultaneously aware of how far we as a people have yet to climb, how much work we have yet to do. And thus we take out our little rubber hammers and bang away; celebrating the great accomplishments of the building of the Jewish State, yet all the while hammering for greater and greater improvement. Site still under construction. Perhaps Moses felt a similar sentiment as he gazed out on the Land so long ago. This poem tries to capture that feeling of arrival and the quest for reaching yet beyond.

A PISGAH PARABLE

Long I climbed
With this peak in mind
Watched it through my hair and sweat
Felt it in my calves and neck
my troubled but determined breath
grew short and tripped
my chapped lips bled

Though body drag
and bloated limb
Attended me in every lift
I bared the wind
As if it was the breathe of God
Upon my neck

And when the path had long turned rock
no longer leaves
but granite block
alone, but for a hoary hawk
aloft above my sleeve
- I stopped

And through the blur of that exhaust
I saw the summit
Long I'd sought

And how I heaved
my body up
to palm the peak
- my summit touched!

And thus I ceased
to celebrate

this vaulted vista
vantage gate
triumphantly as Everest,
as Hillary,
and the nameless rest
drunk on prophecy come true
that one could claim such altitudes
and breathed I deep indeed
my feat

....but brief
for at my back, the hawk did screech

A blade to beckon dare I breach
beyond success
and shallow beach
beyond the patch of skin and stone
that I named "apex"
from below
though climbing had been courage clawed

My findings now
made me give pause
for now from high sight
- rearranged
perspective caught
a vaster mountain range

Not conquered yet
this stump, no steep
but higher still
its reign did reach

A gasp or two
to realize
the throng of peaks
stretched 'fore my eyes

each greater grander than the last

a string of studs
along earth's back

and in that instant
learned I the law
as sure as gravity and awe
Imbibed the truth each climber must:

Tuesday's peak
is Wednesday's dust

IN THE FINAL DAYS

(Poetic Commentary on Parshat Vayehi)

In this week's reading we witness the famous death-bed scene of Jacob calling forth his sons to relay to them what will happen "b'aharit hayamim" in *the final days*. This is the first time in the Torah that we see any reference to the type of messianic visions that will eventually become such a major theme in the prophets and later Jewish thought.

Jacob, though – unlike the prophets, never does give over the details of a messianic vision. His sons gather expectantly to hear the prophecy. And yet, it doesn't come. After his teasing preamble, he turns instead to the topic of blessings for each son. We are left on the edge of our eschatalogical seats. Just as in our present reality, the future remains a dark continent of invisible inevitability.

And yet what is visible in the text that might be revelatory to us? One thing which stands out in Jacob's words is the stress he puts on his sons coming together. "He'asfu," he says, *"Gather together and I will tell you what will be"*. And again in the next verse, he bids them, "Hee'kavtzu v'yishmau". Make of yourselves a group – a *kevutzah* - and hear your father!

For Jacob, it seems that there is something intimately linked about the gathering and the telling, the grouping and the hearing. Indeed, messianic visions by their very nature gather us together, binding our hither-to splintered individual selves into one common narrative, one massive shared drama. Messianism at its best is about unifications, in-gatherings, national and eventually international oneness.

What's more, I would add that it is in our people's very gathering together that the prophecies of the end of time are themselves brought closer to their fulfillment. It is as if we have an inbuilt propensity for gathering, for grouping...some genetically predisposed sense of nationhood, tribe and shared destiny.

The messianic promise in Jacob's words is that when we as individuals make the move from separateness to togetherness, when each of us is able to access the depth and beauty of that sense of being gathered together, bonded in family and fraternity, then the prophetic vision is one person closer to being fulfilled.

I am daily moved by the members of my community who have gathered here in Jerusalem; individuals who are called with an imperative to the fulfillment of our national destiny. Individuals who have chosen to leave behind the comforts and allure of the West, compelled to disentangle from the familiarities of exile, to forge a shared destiny in this complex land.

We who chose to dwell here, to gather here, are – in essence - living on a prophecy. None of us know the details of the end of days, and yet we are drawn together with a sense of its immanence.

The poem below is about that promising immanence of redemption. It is about the cultivation of a sense of shared destiny. Let us gather together, let us celebrate our familial bond, our commonalities. May we gaze in amazement at the ongoing ingathering of the exiles that is occurring before our very eyes and within our very limbs.

DESTINY WE HAVE DANCED

Destiny we have danced
and with the wind of our will
we have wiped away the tears
that our history did spill

and with our hands upon the wheel
that holds our wheels upon the road
we have driven our desire
to our destiny's abode

and though the road stretches far
from creation's first flung light
to the far dark destination
of the future in the night,
we will stop – and take a walk
beneath the sea of stars
catching constellations
in our net of dreams thrown far

for destiny is glimpsed in
and guided by our dreams
while in waking hours
our prayers mix with the reality it brings.

So let me recall a vision to you
of a prayer thrown to an open sky
how our people have watched up after it
with long-enduring yearning eyes

and suddenly it has come back down
and hit the ground before our feet
for fate has come to fulfill the wish
that our dreams had dared to seek

and we are thankful now not only
for the grant of G-d's permission
but for the gift of witnessing
the long path of prayers procession

and thus I come to you
offering this view

of an in-gathering in an instant
of a people living on a prophecy
of community & commitment

and we gather here to witness
the long path of G-d's own dreams
We fulfill G-d's very prayers

with the reality we bring

So let us wander
Yerushalayim together
and raise our thankful eyes
like dreamers our mouths are full of laughter
for the sight which fills the sky

above our heads there blows a vision
we had but beheld in dreams
framed by flickering constellations
a singular blue star beams

It is a prayer shawl upon the wind
for the spirit also prays
It is a sign that day begins

after we've dreamt the night away

I*t is our flag ~*
as fixed as fate and raised on high
it dances with the willful wind
with prayers and dreams
and you
and I

1Like Isaiah spoke, "And it shall come to pass in the last days, that the mountain of the Lord's house shall be established on the top of the mountains, and shall be exalted above the hills, and all the nations shall flow unto it. And many people shall go and say, Come and let us go up to the mountain of the lord, to the house of the God of Jacob; and he will teach us of his ways, and we will walk in his paths: for out of Ziyyon shall go forth Torah, and the word of the Lord from Yerushalayim. And he shall judge among the nations, and shall decide among many people: and they shall beat their swords into plowshares, and their spears into pruning hooks: nation shall not lift up sword against nation, neither shall they learn war any more." (Isaiah 2: 2-4)

ABOUT THE AUTHOR

Chaya Lester is a Jerusalem-based spiritual teacher, psychotherapist, writer and performance artist. She holds an Ivy League BA in Religious Studies, and an MA in Clinical Psychology. She also did extensive doctoral work in Jewish Studies at Oxford University in England.

As co-director of The Shalev Center, for Jewish Personal Growth, she leads seminars and retreats as well as trains and facilitates ongoing women's groups. She is also the creator of "Inner Israel", a spiritual tourism company offering personalized spiritual tours of the Land of Israel to groups of all religious persuasions.

Synthesizing Jewish wisdom, psychology and the arts, Chaya has sculpted an innovative approach to personal transformation & healing. She does this through her teachings & counseling, as well as through her acclaimed one-woman show "Babel's Daughter".

The show traces Chaya's spiritual path from the Bible Belt to the Holy Land. It has been praised as a master-piece by enthusiastic audiences from around the world.

This book takes the script of that show and expands it into a more nuanced and even more electric poetic memoir of Chaya's journey. Although Chaya's trek is a Jewish one, the themes and lessons woven together in this book are universal and reflect an archetypal spiritual quest.

Chaya lives in Nachlaot, Jerusalem with her husband Rabbi Hillel Lester and their three energetic children. Her motto is, "Every mess is Messianic!"

*

Chaya offers private therapy & spiritual counseling in person or via phone and Skype. Please contact the Shalev Center for more information about her counseling services, classes, groups, and show "Babel's Daughter" or if you would like to be added to her mailing list.

Contact info:
Email: Chaya@shalevcenter.org
Phone in Israel: 054-691-8226
Phone in US: 415-412-3344

To learn more visit:
www.chayalester.com

ABOUT THE SHALEV CENTER:

Chaya Lester and her husband Rabbi Hillel are co-founders of the Shalev Center. The Shalev Center's programs turns rich Jewish teachings into relevant and effective vehicles for personal and inter-personal development. Whether through our classes, meditation retreats, on-going groups or private counseling, the Shalev Center gives you the space, the guidance and the tools to go deep and grow.

Please visit us at:
www.shalevcenter.org

Or call:
In the US: 1-415-412-3344
In Israel: 054-691-8226

ABOUT INNER ISRAEL TOURS:

Inner Israel Tours is pioneering the field of Spiritual Tourism in Israel. We create custom spiritual journeys that allow visitors to experience the majesty of Israel on the deepest levels. Our tours transcend mere historical facts & sites on a map. We guide tourists to encounter each sacred site as a portal into sanctifying their own lives.

Through an utterly unique melding of mystical teachings and psychological processing, our trips become truly life-changing journeys. Whatever the religious persuasion of the group, Inner Israel sculpts the tour to fit each groups' precise needs.

For more information please visit:

WWW.INNERISRAEL.ORG

✧

IN PRAISE OF THE SHOW "BABEL'S DAUGHTER"

"Chaya has an unusual combination of talents....the psychological training to enable her to self-reflect and self-reveal, the lyrical flair to put her experiences to verse, and the stage presence to make audiences keen to come along with her for the ride....Her wordplays alone, delivered like an old-new hybrid between a rap and a rapture, are well worth the journey. "
- Ha'aretz (National Israeli newspaper)

"Relating her story in both prose and poetry, Chaya is both entertaining and moving....her show is an intimate way for visitors to experience Israel. People who come to Israel experience an onslaught of historical facts and sites on a map but experiencing Jerusalem can be a deeper inner journey as well."
- Naamat Women Summer 2013 Magazine

"With poetry, humor, and poignant disclosure, Chaya Lester entertainingly wove her personal story, evoking identification, self-revelation, and connection to Torah. Like a fine film, images and insights of *Babel's Daughter* have endured for me contributing to my own unfolding awareness."
- Rabbi Eli Spitz, Orange County

"A Masterpiece! Fun, deep, beautiful, edifying, creative and truly poetic."
-   Sarah Yehudit Schneider, author & teacher

"Chaya's mastery of verbal imagery in a uniquely Jewish context rendered me speechless. As I listened with awe, admiration, and anticipation of each utterance, I had to remind myself to breathe....Chaya's nuanced interpretation of Israel stirs the soul. Chaya educates, entertains and enlivens your inner spark while flaming her own."
-   Gayle Greenhut Schwartz, Haifa Israel

"Chaya Lester's poetry is a gift to our era. Her deep yet soaring interpretations of Judaism bring it alive. Her works will uplift you and connect you in new ways to G-d and the world we live in."
-   Jennifer Laszlo-Mizrahi, Founder of The Israel Project

"It was a great pleasure and honor to have Chaya Lester in our community. Everyone loved the performance. Chaya is a prodigious talent!"
-   Rabbi Wayne Dosick, San Diego CA

"An inspiring journey, eerily identifiable, yet refreshing. A must see for all who are searching, and those who have found and want a taste to remember."
-   Leah Levy, Leah Levy Films

"Chaya is truly a poet and healer using her word wizardry to mend the heart and return it to its divine source. Her show brings the

audience not to her salvation, but to their own. Whether Jewish or not, treat yourself to this soulful journey. You won't regret it."
-   Rachel Kaplan, Berkeley CA

"Chaya Lester's show was a delightful and intense exploration of the Jewish American spiritual journey. While Chaya shares her personal story through hilarious characters, exquisite poetry, and subtle but profound Torah teachings, she invites us to reflect and explore our own journeys. I left the show being moved deeply by reflecting on the wondrous way that God is present in even the most unexpected parts of my life."
-   Rabbi Kvod Wieder, CA

"A most intelligent performance piece on the reality of living the paradoxes of life for us in the Middle East. I highly recommend it to all. Not to be missed!"
-   Rabbi Joe Schonwald, Jerusalem